HANDS 0

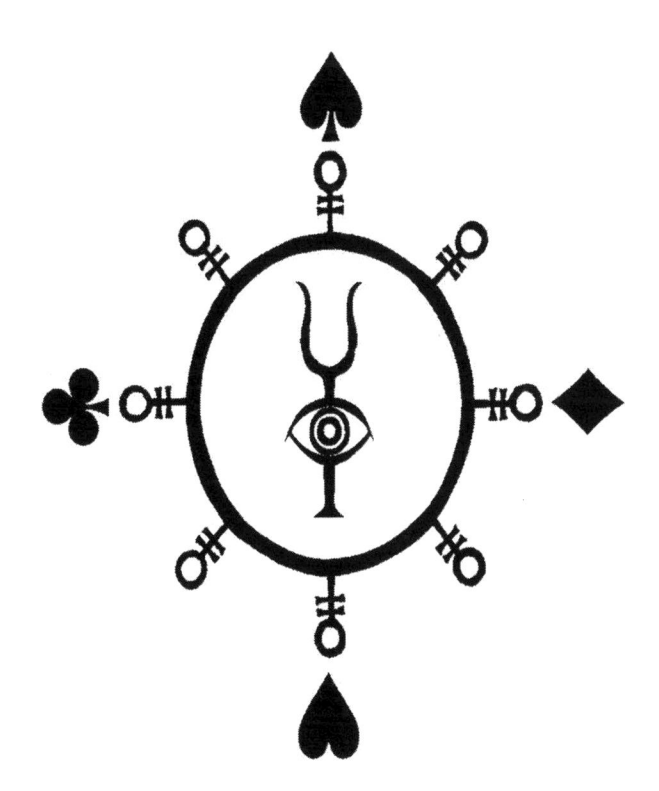

FORTUNUM CITIUS REPERIAS QUAM RETINEAS

HANDS OF FATE
The Art of Divination with Playing Cards

By
Robin Artisson

©2016 Robin Artisson. All rights reserved. This book or parts thereof may not be reproduced in any form, stored in any retrieval system, or transmitted in any form by any means—electronic, mechanical, photocopy, recording, or otherwise—without prior written permission of the publisher, except as provided by United States of America copyright law.

ISBN-13:
978-1530539499
ISBN-10:
1530539498

Black Malkin Press
Algonac, Michigan

www.robinartisson.com

*This work is dedicated to Jean-Baptiste Alliette
and
Marie Anne Adelaide Lenormand,
For all the help they have given me over the years.*

Contents

Introduction, Sorcerous Theory, and Methodologies................................1

A Cunning Method of Cartomancy..18

Meet Now the Persons of the Four Suits..20

These are the Creatures of the Suits...24

Walk now through the World of the Four Suits.....................................25

Now Allow the Hands of Fate to Tell a Tale...33

Sample Fayerie Tale Reading One..36

Sample Fayerie Tale Reading Two...40

The Characters that Spring from the Cards...46

The Atmosphere of the Tale..50

Yes or No for Those Who Must Know...54

Time and the Cards..56

Oracular Pronouncements..58

Whispers of the Soul..61

Death Letter...63

The Table of Major Suit Associations..66

Chart of Basic Card Meanings..69

INTRODUCTION, SORCEROUS THEORY, AND METHODOLOGIES

I. The Provenance of this Work

As a professional cartomancer-diviner, I have studied the art of divination with cards for my entire adult life, and a good portion of the years of my childhood. Though my specialty areas lie in Tarot and Lenormand Piquet divination, the allure of the utilization of ordinary playing cards for divination was always there. In the land of my youth, as with many other lands, diviners often make use of playing cards for acts of fortune telling and prognostication. There is as much occult and mystery-aesthetic surrounding the use of playing cards in this way as any other cartomantic method, and truly, ordinary playing cards have been used longer than either the Tarot or the Lenormand decks for divination. The tradition is venerable and subtle, and very worthy of study.

I have studied various systems of playing card divination; the best sources I have found were in the many playing card divination books written during the latter part of the 19th century, and in the early 20th century (though the 20th century works hearken back, in nearly every case, to much earlier sources. I often encourage people to look into the old vintage oracle and divination books, most often passed off in their own times as "fortune telling" books, for the wealth of old tradition and wisdom that is often found in them. Books like *Madam LeMarchand's Fortune Teller* may be considered quaint and even silly at times, but it, and books like it, hide a wealth of real working insight into what card divination was in previous centuries, and what it still might be.

It was inevitable that I would eventually attempt to systematize my own method for playing card divination based on my research and experiences. I have done this several times, but the work you are presently holding represents my most thorough and serious attempt to do so. This book was, for most of its life, just a file, a notebook, a collection of writings about a method of card divination that I pieced together over time, and through the inspiration won from my esoteric education and experiences as a diviner. Now, I have decided to write a complete introduction to this topic, and talk about the necessary occult technologies or insights required to make card divination "work", and then pass the complete body of that notebook into your keeping.

Thusly armed, you will be able to perform acts of divination that can provide you with extraordinary guidance through the forest of life, or help you to wisely make your way through the dangerous field of our human social world, as the sling-stones and arrows of capricious Fate fall around you. The "notebook" you are about to receive is comprised of many parts, may techniques. You can use them individually, or all together, or in any combination you like.

II. Playing Card Divination in a Very Small Nutshell

As long as there have been playing cards, people have been attempting to use them to divine the future, or gain other insights into the situations of life. Scholars trace the origin of playing cards to the courts of Eastern rulers and potentates, and even in their researches, gazing upon the first playing cards, the "systems" of playing cards reveal their origin in the metaphysical and social underpinnings of ancient societies. The caste system and social system of ancient Persia is reflected in the four suits, and in the "face" cards, or the royals. Numbers have always held mystical significance, even before Pythagoras revealed the underlying occult meanings of numbers, a forged a numerological mysticism that still affects all occultism in the West, and has affected it for every age since he lived.

Even if people had not been using the original playing cards for the sacred or sorcerous purposes of divination, something in the entire institution of playing cards was pregnant with divinatory potential, for our later divinatory card systems- like Tarot- grow directly from them. The idea of using cards for divination is no different, in essence, than the primordial practice of using slips or slats of wood, carved with certain symbols, and cast randomly to gain messages about the future or insights into situations. A playing card, or any card, is just a very thin piece of wood- paper- painted or printed with certain symbols. In shuffle or randomization, certain of those symbols are allowed to come forth to create a message of some sort.

I will discuss it more momentarily, but at this point, I must point out that cards by themselves have no special power. No matter how sacred or meaningful the symbols, pictures, or signs might be that make their way onto the faces of the cards, they are still lacking in any "innate" power. What makes card divination possible is an extraordinary power that grants divinatory messages. That power- which is always a person, whether human or other-than-human- must be a friend to the diviner, or it must be a power that the diviner has access to on some level, before the cards can become an oracle. For it is true now, as it always has been: all true divination is oracular.

The scandalous presence of playing cards throughout the history of Christian Europe is believed by me to be more than the ordinary Christian ascetic disdain for games and merriment, or even for gambling. The "sinful card playing" we hear about through certain eras in history must hide a deep awareness, even if it was not a conscious awareness, that playing cards and acts of divination have an intrinsic and old relationship. When a deck of cards is randomized, and a "hand" is given out from it, stranger forces beyond our comprehension have the opportunity to affect what emerges from the deck. There is a subtle and yet direct conjuration of Fateful powers in this. And what might seem random from one perspective doesn't have to be- and in the case of oracles, nothing is truly random.

The idea that people playing card games are "testing their luck" comes to the forefront of my thinking here. The church, like the Muslim world beyond the borders of Christendom, heavily invested people in the idea that a supreme being secretly and directly controlled all things by his will, eliminating the need for considerations regarding "luck." Luck is by itself a very Heathen concept, an idea that certain people have certain forces playing around them, and within the events of their lives, but not equal forces: some are possessed of more luck-giving powers than others, as the events of their lives reveal.

One way that luck can be known is through how well a person fares at games of chance. This leads to deeper questions about the metaphysical realities of one's life, and perhaps of the world itself, questions that religious authorities from our last batch of centuries would prefer people not consider. Even innocent games of cards offer Fates and strange powers a chance to speak, at a deeper level- and thus, the historical disdain for playing cards is easy to understand, coming from a deeper level.

But far from fleeing the subtle presence of the Fates, the cartomancer must move directly towards it. In the strange world of "randomizing" cards, of turning cards, of revealing Fate's hidden hand, a new engagement with life and the interior depths of life's many events can begin. Divination offers a method of guidance through life's circumstances that is very much outside of the only source of guidance that people in the West and Near East have been allowed to look to: Bishop and Bible, or Mullah and Koran. This is the true "sin" of divination, if ever it had a sin.

III. The Divining Familiar and Sources of Divination

Sorcerers- people who have pacts and relationships with spirits called "familiars"- perform divination through the agency of those familiars. Certain kinds of spirits are especially skilled at, or powerful with regard to giving human beings messages about things that have not yet occurred, or things that are occurring but hard for human beings to comprehend or sense. This is the key to understanding what divination is: it is an attempt to utilize cards or lots or other items to receive messages from the Unseen world, from spirits, which can give clairvoyant or precognitive information about the world as it is.

True divination requires a divining familiar, a spirit that can, for whatever reason, aid humans in the performance of divination. However, sorcery, and the sorcerers that do it, are both rare things these days in the Western world. This does not mean that the ordinary man or woman cannot assay works of divination. It means that the "ordinary" person must connect themselves with a source of divinatory power which they have access to, and fortunately for everyone, the mere fact of being human offers three potential sources of divinatory insight.

For simply being human and having a soul means that underlying connections exist that can be comprehended, and actualized, for the purposes of divination. The man or woman wishing for this will have a small amount of work to do, as they begin to awaken and make those deep portions of themselves active. But it can be done, with a small minimum of effort, by any truly motivated person.

I cannot, in a work of this brevity, go into the deep, dark, and long process that transforms an ordinary person into a sorcerer, into a person who has pacts with familiar powers. But I can offer insight into the three other sources of divinatory connection that I have mentioned here, and give a motivated person all they need to perform divinations through them and by them.

The first of these sources is one's own soul. When I say "one's own soul", I mean to refer to the deeper of the two souls each person possesses- what is often called the free soul or the wandering soul. I do not mean the breath-soul, the soul that vitalizes the body and participates in this world through the act of breathing, which maintains life. I mean the free soul, the soul that makes a person capable of dreams, visions, and deep intuition. I mean the free soul that is our connection to the dark depths of the Unseen World- the Unseen World that is its true home, its origin, and end.

The free soul, being a connecting power between our humanity and the other-than-human powers that exist beyond, can act as a source, a channel, of guidance through divination. And to access it, one must first comprehend that it exists, and give up on all pretenses or hopes that the breath-souled mind, the rational mind, can ever understand what it truly is. At our depths, our most profound layer of being, is the matrix of a deeper connection to the rest of the world, and the spirit-world. At our depths, is a thing, a power, which might be thought in the company of spirits already. This thing, this portion of us, survives our deaths, and pre-existed our births. It is related to another world, and to countless forces in this world, in ways we can't comprehend.

When you sit in a darkened room- and all divination is best done at night or in the dark- and when you relax with yourself, feeling the sensation of your entire body, and let yourself slip into your own depths (a process that happens if you relax and allow it to happen), you reach a quieter, more wordless place, which is the beginning of the road to the free soul, and all the spaces of reality that lie beyond it. If you can learn to sit like this, and ask questions not to the air around you, but directly into the depths of you, and then- most importantly- feel the subtle depths themselves answering you, sometimes in feelings, sometimes in sensations in your very flesh, you can pose questions and ask for guidance from the free soul itself, and all the powers you may not know about who protect your free soul, and may have an interest in guiding you well.

This brings us to the next source of divinatory power that anyone may access: Ancestors. The free souls of men and women who have lived before, and in love and relationship to one another, created children together, or lived alongside one another such that they forged deep connections with one another and their families, still exist.

Though much of who and what they were in their mortal, breathing lives is gone now, the love, connections and other such strong forces they created and were conditioned by in their lives still exist for their descendants, and for people and places they may have been very connected to. Some forces that we encounter or become involved with in our breathing lives impact us not just at the level of the brain or the tissues, but deep enough to change even the soul. Those deep impacts follow us into the world beyond this life, and condition how we will feel and behave even in that place. Thus, the love I have for my children-profound as it is- will surely condition my free soul to do what it can, in the deeper place it occupies after my death, to protect them and my grandchildren and my great-grandchildren, and so forth.

This is the basic rationale for believing in the existence of Ancestral persons and powers who may exert a protective presence in some of our lives. And one of the things they would like to do- and which they do anyway, at times, in dreams- is give us guidance, to help protect us from bad situations, or help us to arrive at good places in our lives. They want us to live not just safely, but well. Thus, if we create a conscious relationship with them, and connect ourselves to them, and then, give them an opportunity to guide us through divination, there is a very high likelihood that they will, in effect, empower us as divining familiars of a very special kind. They do not work for us, giving us divinations in exchange for power or pay; they do it out of love, and what we must do is respect them and love them back for it.

Clearly, if you have parents or grandparents or great-grandparents who have moved through death and into the spirit world already, you have a starting point for creating this special kind of relationship with them, because you already have a potent relationship to them, as loved family. But for the practical purposes of divination, I suggest you take this one step further, with regard to creating the "divinatory connection"- you should obtain soil from their graves, if you can, and keep it in a small black linen or flannel bag.

The dead person and their grave become connected; the free soul and the grave-site become connected. But you cannot just take the earth from the grave; you must ask politely, talk with love to the buried person's soul, and tell them what you need, and why. You have to give offerings for the earth you take- offerings of honey, whiskey or liquor of some sort, wine, or both the honey and the drink. Three copper pennies- pennies minted before 1982- can be given to the ground, right where you took the earth from.

When you take the earth, you leave a hole. You have to "fill the hole" with these offerings, put the offerings in the gap you made, else the grave-earth will not work for you. You must take the earth from the heart or head "level"- from roughly above where the heart or head of the dead person's body is under the ground. Do not take it from anywhere else, and the heart is better than the head for this. The dirt must be tied up in the little bag, and kept in a safe place, untouched by anyone else who wasn't related to the dead person. It is traditional to take the grave-earth at night, but it can be taken in the day, particularly at dawn or in the late afternoon.

The little bag must be "fed"- a dab of wine or whiskey or liquor of some sort should be given to it, pushed right into it with your finger, before each use. This earth connects you to the relative or Ancestor, and it does something else, too. Through them, it connects you to your entire family-line that extend out from "behind" them and disappears into the deep mists of the past. This is an enormously powerful talisman that has to be treated with respect.

You can make more than one bag. You can have several, for several relatives, and you can store them all together. They must all be fed at each use. To divine with them, you take them out, at night, by candlelight or firelight, and you "feed" each one. Then, you hold them in your hands and breathe into them, mixing your breath-soul with the earth, and talk to them, telling them what you desire. You may experience yourself as only talking to bags of earth, but you must *feel* and *know* that you are also talking to the souls of the dead- not just the relatives you might have known, but many grandmothers and grandfathers you don't know, who may sense this event on some level.

Then, you must tap the bags against the deck you are going to use for the divination, and then proceed with your divinatory method. Keep the bags at the table while you randomize your cards and read them. Try to "feel" deep down into your own soul, as described before, while you do this, for that is the "place" wherein the Ancestors will communicate with you.

* * *

The third source of divinatory power is by far the most unusual and even frightening, to some. The Prince of the Dark himself, the Master of Spirits in the Unseen World, has a special relationship to humankind. Through the intermediaries of his serving-spirits, he can be appealed to, for help in divinations. The method of reaching out to him, however, has no special technique or science behind it. This is the work of the strange and lonely soul, your own deep desire reaching out to embrace him to find him in the darkness beyond this world, and ask for his help.

Lighting a candle in a darkened room and meditating on the image of a great dark being in a dense, shadowed forest somewhere far to the left of you and beyond our ordinary world as though it were on the other side of an invisible wall, or meditating on the same image yet sensing it as being somehow far behind you, is a good starting point. For a drop of your blood, drawn from one of the fingers of your left hand and smeared upon the candle you are burning, the Master-Spirit may aid you in divination, or send one of his servitor spirits to do the same. There can be no assurances with this method, but for the special soul that feels His power, it might be thought the best method of all. Naturally, I would suggest blending all three of these sources of power together, on whatever level you can, when doing divinations if you lack a Divining Familiar.

There are a few other minor points I should mention now. If you are working only with your free soul as the source of your divinations, try to work only at night, and only when the moon is in a watery house- the houses of Cancer, Scorpio, and Pisces. But you may work on a full moon or a new moon no matter what house it is in. You can divine "against" this moon-rule, but following it will add accuracy, ineluctably, to your work.

If you are using the Ancestral method I have detailed here, you can read at any time you like, though it's still best done at night. If you feel that you are connected strongly to a divine being or some religious icon, if you are religious in this sense, and you believe that just praying for help is enough to gain good divinations, I would still suggest that you only do these "devotionally guided" divinations when the moon is in a watery or airy house (the air-associated houses are the houses of Gemini, Libra, and Aquarius) and still, only at night.

If you utilize only the third of the methods I talked about, reaching out to the Master Spirit for aid, you can again, divine at whatever time you feel his presence allows for it. There is one more small hint here- if you are ever, for some reason, divining about when another person will die, or (more curiously) when you yourself may die, that kind of divination about such rare and deep information is best done when the moon is in the house of Scorpio.

IV. Rules of Divination and Basic Method

When consulting an oracle, there are three very important rules that must be adhered to at all times, if you wish to maintain a respectful and fruitful working relationship, and maintain accuracy in your readings. The first of these rules is "Do not ask for an answer to a question you already know the answer to." This implies mistrust of the oracle, and will destroy your working relationship with it. The second is "Do not ask the same question twice." You receive the answer you were intended to receive, if your working relationship is a good one. You must wait for a significant amount of time before you ask a question again, or wait until forces, situations, and factors in your life-situation have changed significantly, before you can ask again.

The third rule is "Do not ask questions that you don't really want to know the answer to." There is an important wisdom here; knowing too much about too many things can destroy your personal happiness or ability to have peace of mind. This also means that you should never ask frivolous questions, or questions that have answers which can be obtained through easier methods. Divination is for extra-difficult or dense situations in which extraordinary insight or knowledge is really needed to help find your way to clarity or good strategies for moving ahead. Divination is for "seeing around the corners" that we cannot ordinarily see around, so that we can be forewarned of possible trials or dangers, and prepare for them. Divination is also for self-knowledge, for knowledge of deeper things that you need to guide you.

If you choose to engage divination as a diviner, there is one more traditional "rule" that you might want to adhere to: once your soul and your body have been used to engage sacred or powerful things like divination through cards, once you have used cards in this manner, you must abstain from playing serious card games or gambling for money, using cards. Your relationship with the cards themselves- understanding as you will what an important connective role they have between humans and the deeper, more potent world beyond ordinary human considerations- should render you unwilling to use the cards for frivolous purposes.

Reading for yourself is straightforward, though you must be in possession of a lot of self-awareness and brutal self-honesty if you want to obtain accurate answers. I suggest that you have others read for you in very dense or troubling situations, in which your objectivity will be suspect. However, reading for other people is a more nuanced matter. If another gives you permission to read for them, and explains the situation in detail that they wish to be subjected to divinatory work, all is well. But if you wish to pry into the life-situations and realities of other persons without their knowledge or permission, you will run into the problem of their own soul and the powers that surround them possibly rejecting your attempt.

To gain insight into the lives or minds of other people, you will have to make special sacrifices. The information you seek doesn't belong to you, and in effect, you are spying or even attempting a theft of types. This is not true if you are reading about a situation that involves both you and them- such as reading about how your employer may react to a new thing you've done, or will do. But if you don't relate to the situation, and simply seek deeper information of this kind about another, you will have to do something special and painful or expensive to obtain it.

Nothing less than the shedding of blood from your left hand- or something else as intimate and painful- will make it possible. Giving up something very precious or expensive, destroying or burying or somehow parting yourself from this thing in some permanent way may also do the trick, as it were. You are attempting to bribe the fateful powers that surround that person into giving you the information you seek. Think carefully on this.

When you read for another- with their permission or not- you need to be able to identify the subject of your reading to your divining familiar or the source of your divination. You must know their names, first and last, and it really helps if you know their mother's first name and maiden name, too. When you ask questions about them, or on their behalf, try to identify them as "Jane Smith whom Janet Thomas bore." That is the ideal method of identifying another to the Unseen.

When you do your readings, always begin by getting into contact with the sources of your divination- divining familiars, if you have them, or one or all of the three sources that anyone can access, as I described herein. Then, when you feel the strong presence or connection to those powers, speak out loud and "towards" those powers, or within to yourself. Ask the question very clearly.

Then, when you are ready, when you have phrased the question to your satisfaction, lay out seven cards from your deck before you, face down. Without thinking about what you are doing, begin laying down cards from the deck in your hand onto those seven, randomly putting a card onto any of the seven cards laying before you. You will create seven stacks of cards by the time you are done. Pick up the seven stacks randomly, and then cut once, as close to the center as you can, but don't think about that overly much, either.

When you have done this, you have randomized. The reading is ready; the card now on top, and those that follow it, are the message the source of your divination has "stacked" for you, using your hands and body. Always randomize this way.

V. Light Joker, Dark Joker, and Suggested Decks for Reading

When you obtain a deck for divination, make sure that it has two jokers, and further (as is traditional in most decks) be sure that the two jokers can be told apart- one will be a "light joker" and the other will be the "dark joker" (which I also call "the Thief.") Bicycle, the most prominent and popular manufacturer of playing card decks, often show one Joker as just a king riding a bike, and the other as a smaller image of the king on a bike, with the words "Guarantee" below it, followed by their pledge to guarantee the quality of the deck. The "Guarantee" Joker is the light joker in an ordinary Bicycle deck. The other one is the dark joker.

Other decks will have many kinds of jokers, and most will alter the image of one so that it stands out from the other. You must associate one with light, and the other with dark. I strongly suggest the following decks as in keeping with the mystical aesthetic of playing card divination. Please obtain one or several and use them, though truly, any deck can be used.

-The Expert Playing Card Company "Joker and the Thief" deck: this is the deck I suggest. It has a beautiful Victorian aesthetic, with much occult detail and a dark joker who is called "The Thief" by the deck itself. This system I am about to share with you in this book utilizes this deck as its "standard."

-The Bicycle "Ghost" deck made by the Ellusionist Playing Card Company

-The "Infinity" deck made by the Ellusionist Playing Card Company

-The "Arcane" deck made by the Ellusionist Playing Card Company

-The Bicycle "Expert Back" playing card deck

* * *

With all of the information I have presented here, you have all that you need to access and utilize the book I am about to present to you in the next section. Read through it, and make of it what you will and can. I wish you much luck and accuracy in your divinatory efforts.

THE COMPLETE TEXT OF "HANDS OF FATE."

I. Good Day and Listen close to me; I detail a Cunning Method of Cartomancy.

The suits of ordinary cards, you know already- but to see with me, understand them anew.

Spades are **Elf Arrows**, the signs of the predatory powers that come and take from the world- they fly unseen and they kill animal and beast, but ruin forest, city and civilization, too. They are woes, illnesses, deaths, conflicts and foes. The Elves are the Fayerie-People, the spirits of the dead. The Elf-Arrows represent the Breath Soul's divisive cunning and manipulations. This suit encompasses the winds of the world, and all atmospheric phenomenon. This suit is aligned with winter.

Hearts are **Desires**, the signs of all that is warm and loving to you- they mean emotions and love, but they also refer to those closest to you- the family you hold dear, but also friends, allies, lovers, and desired ones. They are the feelings and deep textures of the Wandering Soul, connected to visions and stranger things, too. This suit encompasses the waters of the world, and the watery abyss below the earth. This suit is aligned with Autumn.

Clubs are **Trees**, the trees of a great forest, the forest of life- they mean the actions you must and will take in this forest of life, and the landscape your actions take place upon, and the other persons- not so close to you, even strangers- you may meet. The Trees are things occurring, as the wind makes the trees move and sway; they are activities, your will to act and interact. They are the Breath Soul's animating power and drive. This suit encompasses the fiery energy generated when things interact, whether through friction or cooperation. This suit is aligned with Spring.

Diamonds are **Coins**, the valuable items and powers you need to live and make your way in the world. They are all that is necessary- money, food, houses, clothes- but also the health of the body which is the soul's house in manifestation. They are tangible things, including money- and though our money is very much fake, it can be traded for things that are quite real. The coins suit speaks to sustenance and safety, comfort and solidity. This suit encompasses the mineral presence of the earth itself. This suit is aligned with Summer.

II. Meet Now the Persons of the Four Suits

KING OF SPADES: Esuric, the King of Elf-Arrows, Leader of the Wild Host of Arrow-Shooting Fates. He is the Stormer, the Leader of the Storm, the great and lethal one. His character is severe and can be pitiless. He means vengeance and true justice; he upsets and lays waste to any state of affairs that is not fatefully protected. He is the source of winds and breath souls, the teacher of sorcerous words and works.

QUEEN OF SPADES: Beira, Nicneven, the Queen of Elf-Arrows, Wife of the Huntsman, Queen of Storms, Queen of Winter, the Scathing One- She is the bringer of difficulties, of criticism and anxiety.

JACK OF SPADES: Cathoc, the Hobb of Elf-Arrows, The Daimon of Injuries and Dangers, the Ill Wind, he is your enemy or enemies, a stalker, a foe, a misfortune, a killer, and possibly a traitor.

* * *

KING OF HEARTS: Unguwen, the King of Desires, The Old Serpent, the Wise Old One, Mighty in Counsel, Lord of Dreams, Interpreter of Visions, Shower of the Way of Wisdom. He is the very essence of wisdom, good counsel, and understanding.

QUEEN OF HEARTS: Ilara, the Queen of Desires, Great Dame Venus, Habondia, the Rose Queen, the Venusian Queen of all Life. She is the power of allure and love, which fills all things with wonder, but has a terrible face, too, for love enslaves, ensnares, and compels to madness and harm at times. She is pleasure incarnate, and addiction.

JACK OF HEARTS: Aros, the Hobb of Desires, the Daimon-Lover, the Seducer. He is the image of the Lothario or the Don Juan, the lover, seducer, and the manipulator, too, for none are more manipulative than he. His promises more often than not turn to fayerie dust in the morning light. But he can give joy in the short term that is nearly peerless.

* * *

KING OF CLUBS: Cunamac, the King of the Forest, Old Hobb, Wild One, The Horned Master of Beasts, Lord of the Hobbs, The Ancient One. He is the leader of living things, and none lead better than he because he leads from the deep, from inside of flesh and blood. He compels all things to move in their time and fashion. All life is under his warding hand. He is leadership, and protection. He is vitality, the organic power of living beings.

QUEEN OF CLUBS: Bremo, the Queen of the Forest, Surrounded by Deer as Her Handmaids and Serving Men, Queen of the Hobbs, Wild Lady, Possessed of Great Power. She is the one who achieves all things, for she has the strength and resources of the whole forest of life at her disposal. She is achievement and connection, full of the same great vitality as her husband.

JACK OF CLUBS: Oryon, the Hobb of the Forest, horned, randy, and twisted- the Daimon of Nature's Depths, the Wild Spirit of deserted places and dense growth. He knows all things beyond the pale of civilized maps and charts; he is the great guide, and always he is adventuring, wandering, taking risks. He is risk; he is guidance, he is adventure, which isn't always safe- or perhaps seldom is.

* * *

KING OF DIAMONDS: Kadrus, the King of the Underworld and all its wealth, King of the Dead. Precious stones hang from his dark horns. He mediates all the bounty of the World Below, source of all life, so none are more generous than he. He is Wealth and Generosity incarnate. He is all powers that keep or guard wealth, whether they be generous or no.

QUEEN OF DIAMONDS: Cuda, the Queen of the Underworld, Indweller in the Earth. She is the Mother of All Life, the Great Grandmother of Wandering Souls. She is the origin of all wealth and things needed for life. She is the origin of life. She is the image of Abundance, and Nurturing. She means "origin" and she means "ending", too, at the same time.

JACK OF DIAMONDS: Dusioc, the Hobb of Coins, The Spirit of the Golden Fields, Daimon of the Hearth, Tavern, Ale-Cup, and Bee-Hive. He is very care-free, for all the wealth and vital powers of nature fall through his hands easily- he is the free one, the gambler, often irresponsible, sometimes a thief, for he loves to acquire things and receive gifts. He can be the con or the fraud- any deceit to gain more golden treasures. He is the image of irresponsible, carefree or thoughtless unpredictability- just as wealth itself is unpredictable.

* * *

THE LIGHT JOKER: The joker, the jester, the jovial one- he represents the good and helpful spirits of the Unseen, even one's familiars, who may enter any situation to help and aid you. They protect and give luck in any situation. If they appear next to a woeful card, they mitigate its woes, sometimes altogether. If they appear between two woeful cards, they mitigate the one that is more severe than the other. If they appear next to a joyful card, they magnify its impact, and if they appear between two joyful cards, they make the better of the two much better.

THE DARK JOKER or THE THIEF: The Thief is a malevolent spiritual power of the Unseen that may appears into a situation to take from you, or to twist and warp circumstances to your great misfortune. He ruins what you thought was surely good and safe. If the Thief appears next to a joyful card, he steals its joy, sometimes completely. If the Thief appears between two joyful cards, he steals the positive impact of whichever is more joyful. If he appears next to a woeful card, he magnifies its effect. If he appears between two woeful cards, he makes the worse of the two much worse. If the Joker and Thief appear together (side by side or around a card), they cancel one another out.

III. These are the Creatures of the Suits

Spades: Owls, Crows/Ravens, Hawks, Eagles, Dogs, Wolves, Spiders, Vultures, Buzzards

Hearts: Cats, Toads/Frogs, Hares, Moth, Butterflies, Ducks, Geese, Swans, Fish, Peacocks

Clubs: Deer, Antlered Beasts, Rams, Squirrels, Rats/Mice, Stoats, Weasels, Foxes, Robins, Crickets, Ladybugs, Raccoons

Diamonds: Goats, Cows/Bulls, Serpents, Lizards, Pigs/Boar, Horses, Bees, Wrens, Badgers, Bear, Ants, Beetles, Turtles, Bats

IV. Walk Now through the World of the Four Suits

ELF ARROWS

A: The Ace of Spades/Elf Arrows means Death and Change. It is the single Elf-Arrow flying to destroy or change something.

2: The Two of Elf Arrows means a Duel, or a Fight. The two arrows on the card face off against one another. It can mean disputes and arguments, too.

3. The Three of Elf Arrows means a Wound has been inflicted; between the two arrows on the card, the two blades of the duelists, the third arrow appears as the injury. This wound is terrifically painful or otherwise inconvenient or hurtful, but can be survived.

4. The Four of Elf Arrows means Peace- the center of the card is clear, but four arrows are arranged around that open center, that peaceful place. Conflict is never far from this peace, yet peace it is.

5. The Five of Elf Arrows means Mortal Injury- a wound that will kill has landed. It also means Terror and Fear.

6. The Six of Elf Arrows shows the Safe Path. Though arrows fall on both sides of the Path, (three to either side of it, on the card) the way down the center is clear. Safety and caution are shown. Movement and travel is presaged, as is change.

7. The Seven of Elf Arrows shows a group five arrows on one side of the card, and two on another- and thus, it is an image of being stuck between the Mortal Injury of

Five, and the Conflict of Two- it is an image of being delayed or stuck, unable to move without harm- or perhaps facing the choice between the lesser of two evils. "Between a rock and a hard place."

8. The Eight of Elf-Arrows is a sign of being frozen, imprisoned, or trapped. Though the center of the card is clear, outside of the square formed by the dangerous arrows await only fights- pairs of arrows- above it and below it. There is no way to leave easily.

9. The Nine of Elf Arrows shows the Funeral Road, with the coffin going down its center. It is a card of funerals, of mourning, of the coffins we put our dearly departed within before parting with them forever, and of ghosts. It is a card of regrets. It is a card of endings and closures and stoppage.

10. The Ten of Elf Arrows shows a Graveyard or a Battlefield freshly piled with the slain. It is a card of Ruin and Decay, a ground peppered full of arrows. It is desolation and silence. It can mean greed, too.

DESIRES

A: The Ace of Hearts/Desires shows two possibilities: It shows a lonely heart, and thus loneliness, or it shows a new love or passion- the sorcery of the new passion or desire which fills all with endless motivation. It can also mean innocence and naivety at times.

2: The Two of Desires shows two hearts interacting together. They gaze across at one another; they mean attraction, sex, interaction, and friendship. This is a card of friendly negotiation, exchange, or interaction. It is a talkative card, of discussions and even chatters. It may mean trickery.

3: The Three of Desires shows that the two hearts have been joined by a third- the third represents a stable love, a stable relationship, and beauty.

4: The Four of Desires shows an empty space at the center of the card, the open, empty space wherein feelings and emotions cool down and even become boring. Though hearts are all around the empty space, they are no longer at the center of a person's mind or attention. This card is stable, but perhaps too stable, such as to lead to boredom or listlessness. It also means "decrease."

5. The Five of Desires is the card of heartbreak, the mortal wound of the soul. It is chief among all things sad.

6. The Six of Desires shows the happy "Rose Road"- both sides of the road decorated with the symbols of Venusian grace. It means happy progress and fruitful relations with

others. It means "flow" and inspiration. It means migration, and change.

7. The Seven of Desires shows the unfortunate place a person may be in from time to time, between heartbreak on the one hand (five hearts), and the possibility of new love, or sex, or attraction on the other (two hearts). It is a card that means "wavering"- to waver in one's feelings or motivations. It can mean disquiet, depression, and betrayal; it means a lack of ability to trust.

8. The Eight of Desires shows that the space of a relationship (the four diamonds in the center) is surrounded by pairs of hearts, meaning love and attraction, above it and below it- it is a card of a Healthy, strong relationship. It means loyalty and emotional well-being. It is Idyllic.

9. The Nine of Desires shows two things: a long, merrily decorated wedding aisle, with a bride walking down it, or a birth-canal, with a child proceeding down it to birth. It is a card of happiness. It refers to unions, agreements, and alliances, too.

10. The Ten of Desires shows The Rose Queen's Bower: the place of comfort, dreams, and bliss. It is the card of the happiest ending, but it conceals a danger, of becoming enamored and sidetracked by pleasures and lost to feelings that other concerns- perhaps even important ones- cannot penetrate. This card can mean some of the best happiness or rest, but it can also mean loss of perspective.

TREES

A: The Ace of Clubs/Trees shows a person alone in a forest. It means solitude, but it also means a deep urge to explore.

2: The Two of Trees shows two sticks being rubbed together, to make warmth and fire. It means constructive or productive effort, but also meeting an ally and making an ally- it means a pact or agreement.

3. The Three of Threes shows a hedge, or a wall. It means obstacle or blockage.

4. The Four of Trees shows a clearing, a field- the center of the card is empty, open, but surrounded at its four points by trees and growth. This means "clearness" and "unobstructed way"- but it also means reaping, what must be harvested, or what was harvested.

5. The Five of Trees is the card of failure. Efforts are lost to failure, to outcomes not desired. In the center of the clearing made by the four other trees, the stump that could not be removed is shown.

6. The Six of Trees shows the track, the pathway through the forest. On either side of it are trees, but the way is clear, and can be seen. This card means that one can or will find their way, and it means progress and perhaps a journey or a movement of some kind. It is the card of teaching, learning, and guidance.

7. The Seven of Trees shows the indecisive place a person may be between failure, and the need to try again or make great effort again- between the five clubs that are

on the card, and the two that are under that five. This means indecision, confusion, and frustration. It also means "becoming lost in the forest."

8. The Eight of Trees shows a clearing at the center, but on either side of it, two trees interact- activities are going on around this still center. You, standing at the center, once acted in those ways, but have learned much. You can observe now, even teach if needs be. This is a card of wisdom and experience gained. It is a card of expertise and understanding. It means achievement and honors, too.

9. The Nine of Trees shows a thicket, a dense thicket in the forest, which means a loss of clarity, an inability to see ahead, and an obstacle.

10. The Ten of Trees shows a clearing at the center of a great forest; this is the image of the great forest, a card full of trees. It means that all actions are done, and now is the time of rest- for it often means that you or another are spent, exhausted, finally unable to do much more. It is a card of the regeneration that will come soon, or one day. The Great Forest shelters- you are safe in it, but you cannot leave it easily, either, so it can mean a final limitation.

COINS

A: The Ace of Diamonds/Coins is the image of a coin, or a letter. Whichever it is, it means a true opportunity to gain, perhaps quite greatly. It also means news or a message.

2: The Two of Coins means exchange- the two coins fly back and forth on the card, and this is the card of transactions, of choices, and visits to others. It can mean gossip and rumors, too.

3. The Three of Coins means that between the exchange, a solid thing has appeared- a job, an acquisition, employment, or something that leads to growing gain. It can mean acquisitiveness and greed, too.

4. The Four of Coins shows a table; clear in the center, with four sturdy legs. The table is still, and this card says "things do not change much." It means stability. It can refer to a store or a shop, too, or a dinner or feasting table that has enough.

5. The Five of Coins shows the ugliest thing of all: poverty, poorness and want. It means loss and sadness. It is a card not just of poverty, but of ugly things, ugly people or offensive-looking places. Not all ugliness is exterior. The poverty of the soul leads to another sort of ugliness, in interaction between people.

6. The Six of Coins shows the "Golden Road"- an open way, a street paved with gold, with coins strewn to either side of it. It means sustenance, provision, and plenty.

7. The Seven of Coins shows a person situated between poverty or loss on the one hand, and the painful need to

make new offers or new exchanges to start all over again on the other. It is a card of disappointment and despair, and it can mean loss of valuable things or theft, too.

8. The Eight of Coins shows a sturdy castle, strong and rich, and it means strength, assurances, and defense or safety. It can also refer to things kept secret or concealed.

9. The Nine of Coins shows a splendid court, the lords and ladies all gathered to one side of it, or the other, with a richly-dressed king or queen walking down the center aisle between them. It also shows a coin inside of a very rich treasury. Either way, it means abundance and power. It means authority, too.

10. The Ten of Coins is the Cavern of Precious Stones, the cavern of the Underworld itself, from whence all riches come. It means endless bounty, and wonder. Or it may refer to a lasting situation, or many of something. It is a storehouse; it is a horde; it is an archive or a library or a great collection of anything, even the collection of the dead in the underworld. It can also mean "much" or "great quantity."

V. Now Allow the Hands of Fate to Tell a Tale

This method of cartomancy is a *story catcher*; it creates stories to answer your questions or offer you guidance. It allows the Free Soul to communicate tales and narratives with many layers. Once you have rightly paid your Divining Familiar for its guidance or aid, cut the well-randomized deck and turn over the top card.

If that card is the Joker, the Thief, or any Ace, you will be answered with a **Fireside Tale**.

If that card is any numbered card from 2 to 10, you will be answered with a **Fayerie Tale**.

If that card is any King, Queen, or Jack, you will be answered with an **Epic Tale**.

Return that card to the deck, and shuffle once more, cut once more, and turn over six cards for a Fireside Tale, nine cards for a fayerie tale, and twelve cards for an epic tale.

Lay them before you in groups of three, in the order that they were drawn- each group of three will be one part of the story. Scan what you see: if any Kings, Queens, or Jacks have been drawn, you must turn over another card and place it under them- that is the card of their character, revealing what their motivation is, what they bring, what they do in this story.

Once you have done this, read your story. Let the cards guide you. Several detailed examples are given below. The character of the story can be marked with many tragedies, or many good occurrences- all signs presaging how things will unfold with a situation in question. It may reveal surprise turns, or dangerous persons. These apply to the situation being read about.

At the end of the story, the cards will have one more method of revealing answers to specific questions- The first three cards reveal something of the querent's **personal fortunes** or well-being in the situation they may be asking about; the second three represent their **relational fortunes** as they deal with others, and the third three cards reveal their **tangible fortunes**, if money or property or health is being inquired about. Tangible fortunes also speak to their environment.

Fireside tales (which only have two sets of three cards) offer no extra information about tangible fortunes beyond what will be divined from the story. Epic tales offer a fourth extra set of information- the fourth set of three cards reveals **unseen fortunes**, a profile of the dominant current unseen powers acting on the situation in question, powers which might be understood, dealt with or bargained with in other ways.

Though an entire story may have had many troubling elements, if one of these "fortune tellings"- the three cards dealing with personal fortunes, or tangible fortunes, or whatever- are positive, then they mitigate (at least on the specific level they speak to) the troubling effect of the story's darker points.

In other words, though a story may end very poorly, if the three cards referring to a person's relationship fortunes are good, then in the "real world" situation they were reading about, they can trust that their interpersonal relationships will not be the primary things punished or harmed.

Bear in mind that when you are looking at the "sets of three" to divine things like the relational fortunes or the personal fortunes, or whatever, that character cards drawn to modify kings, queens, and jacks, are not counted or considered with regard to the meanings of the three cards.

SAMPLE FAYERIE TALE READING ONE
First Three Cards
Jeannie was quite unhappy, living in great poverty. (Five of Diamonds)

One day, walking down the road, she encountered a being of great power who had much wise counsel for her. (King of Hearts) He told her that he could free her from what tormented her, open up her life, clear away the things that troubled her (His character card: Four of Clubs.)

She eagerly went with him, and he led her into the heart of a Great Forest (10 of Clubs.)

Second Three Cards
She looked around, and discovered that she was alone; he had vanished. So she began to explore. (Ace of Clubs)

Lo and behold, in this deep forest, she came across the dark and mighty King of the Underworld himself (King of Diamonds) He was on an adventure of his own, but he offered to be her guide, but he warned her there might be risks. (His character card: Jack of Clubs.)

He led her to a great and majestic Castle. (Eight of Diamonds.)

Third Three Cards
Jeannie discovered that this castle was no friendly place- the dark hosts of the castle placed her in great danger- showing her terrible visions of dangers that she was forced to choose between, though no outcome seemed a good one. (Seven of Spades)

In the middle of her torment, the Wise Stranger appeared to Jeannie again, to show her that the dangers she was being forced to confront were only reflections of her inner life, of things in her soul: the betrayal she had suffered at the hands of another, and her inability to trust

others because of it, had brought her to the poor state she was in at the story's beginning. (Seven of Hearts)
Upon realizing these things, Jeannie was freed from the castle, and returned to her home with her heart healed. (Eight of Hearts.)

Usually, when the final card of a story is positive, the story has a happy ending, but that's not a rule that holds true at all times. In the case of this sample story, I felt the two sevens that appeared next to one another were begging for the relationship I drew between them- many other storytellers, guided in that moment of divination by other powers, might tell a very different tale of what the two sevens meant to Jeannie in the castle. Things could have gone harder for her, but it would have been difficult- and against the cards- to end this story too darkly, considering the "ending" card is the Eight of Hearts, a very positive card in this way of reading.

This sample reading also yields the following:

Personal Fortunes: Five of Diamonds, King of Hearts, Ten of Clubs: poverty, wise counsel, exhaustion/limitations- relatively negative signs here. It seems that a person's individual emotional course through this situation will be hard, though they will have a good friend or some wise counsel from somewhere to help them, but it will still be exhausting.

To form an actual sentence from the three cards can yield a darker outcome: "Impoverished wisdom leads to Exhaustion"- or a lighter one: "Impoverished Wisdom becomes Exhausted." Any such attempts to form messages must be guided by one's own familiar, one's own intuition, in the moment of the reading.

Relational Fortunes: Ace of Clubs, King of Diamonds, Eight of Diamonds: Loneliness, Generosity, Assurances or Safety. Mostly good- What begins slow for relational life ends quite well.

Tangible Fortunes: Seven of Spades, Seven of Hearts, Eight of Hearts: Stuck, Wavering/Depression, and Emotional Well-Being: Though in the long-run, a person will end up okay tangibly speaking, it will be a long hard road to get there, without much success or largesse along the way.

If this reading had been about answering someone's question regarding how they were going to do integrating socially with a new job-site and a new company, the story itself reveals that they would start out (as we knew) not knowing anyone (impoverished, at that level) and would meet someone very important, soon into their new job, that would be able to help them greatly, to lead them into the "Forest" of the company- and they would have some difficulties at first, making close contacts- finding themselves alone in that forest, they would be met with a lot of generosity on the parts of people there, and find a lot of stability (the castle) in this regard.

When problems did come- and come they will- the querent would need to know that the issues would end well if they could understand the role their own history and personality plays in interaction, and be willing to try to trust people or make personal changes in themselves to try new strategies. Because if they did that, they would get the happy ending- friends or allies a-plenty at this place.

This is held up by their three "Relational Cards"- which as we have already seen read "What begins slow for relational life ends quite well."

SAMPLE FAYERIE TALE READING TWO

Cards Drawn:

First Three: Two of Hearts, Five of Spades, Five of Hearts.

Second Three: King of Hearts (Character: Five of Diamonds), Queen of Clubs (Character: Three of Spades), and Four of Clubs

Third Three: Jack of Spades (Character: Eight of Diamonds), Nine of Clubs, Ten of Diamonds

From these cards, the following story was told. Read through it, and look back to the cards selected to see if you can tell how the cards shaped the story-parts.

* * *

"This is a story about two people in love- I can't say if they were the world's greatest all-time lovers, but their two hearts were surely communicating, flirting, attracted to one another. One day, one of them- the woman, I think- was walking along a fence-line, near to the evening, on the corner of the village in which she lived, when a terrible thing happened. A fayerie-arrow cut through the air, invisibly, and mortally wounded her soul. This is grim, for it means that she will surely die in a short time, if her soul is fatally harmed, as hers was. And though she might not have known what had occurred- for the Elf-Arrows fly in a fatefully invisible world, obscure to human senses, she felt a great heartbreak overwhelm her. Her soul knew, even if she did not, that the wound it had received was fatal. She knew she'd be parted from her love, deep down.

She lost her connection to the village where she lived; these supernatural events and their impact on her depths were too great, so she slumped down, and just lost consciousness for a while. She awoke late at night, and decided to climb under the fence, and walk off into the forest. She was doing with her body and what was left of her life-force what her soul was going to do anyway.

So off she went into the forest. And several hours after wandering aimlessly among the trees, she encountered an old man- a strange old man, who could not possibly have lived there. Old, bent, and hoary he was- but he had a vitality that marked him as something other-than-human. He was the Master of Secret Wisdom, a teacher and counselor sought by many in the human world, but seldom found. Here, this girl had found him, without even trying to look. Was there any wisdom in the world that could save a person in her wretched condition? Could wisdom reverse such a cruel outcome of Fate as she had fallen victim to?

If the Old Master was able to help her- and she surely asked- he was prevented by his own need. "Look at me", he told her- "Look at my mean condition- rags draped over my bones, and my limbs have become skinny from hunger. Can you help me in return for what I might tell you, Dead Girl?" That's what he said to her. Such is the terrible condition of our world that the Master of Wisdom himself lives in poverty. The girl said that she would get good clothing and food for him, and she wandered further away in the forest.

And lo, and behold, as the night was rolling on, seeming so endless, she encountered another powerful being- this time, it was the Queen of the Wild Forest herself; she wasn't even trying to seem human; she was majestic, surrounded by deer and hares and boar, her long brown, wavy hair falling all the way to her knees, draping her naked form like clothing.

Our heroine asked the Queen of the Wild if she could help her to rescue the Master of Wisdom from his plight, and our Heroine got more bad news- the Queen would have been happy to help her, if not for her injury. Our Heroine then noticed the bloody matted hair on the Queen's breast, and saw that she was, indeed, injured. A human poacher had fired upon one of her deer, but the shot had gone stray and struck her. Her magic took the life of the poacher, but his wound still persisted in her. "If you can get me the wort I need to staunch this wound and heal it, I will help you" the Queen told her. The Queen said that there was a clearing not far from there with the herb in it, and off our heroine went.

The clearing was there, as the Queen said it would be. And along its edges, different herbs swayed. She saw the one she needed.

She proceeded to obtain it, when a dark figure appeared between she and it. He was dark-eyed, lithe, and pitiless to the last- he was the entity that had shot the Elf-arrow that had killed her soul that evening. He had a collection of other cruel Elf-Arrows, and a fine hunting bow, and a curved-bladed knife. "I shot you, and I killed you" he said. "And yet, here you are, no longer alive, but not yet dead, tromping through the forest, making bargains with beings far your superior, and far beyond your comprehension, thinking to undo what hard Fate has decided."

Oddly enough, the girl hadn't even considered that she was doing this- she was too heartbroken to really think about her ultimate motivations. She was lost in her brokenness, lost in her approaching death. The more she thought about it, the more she couldn't arouse the energy to continue to care about these tasks she found herself set to.

She tried to get past the Hunter of Souls, but he easily repelled her attempts to reach the healing herb. "I protect the things here" he said. "They're not for your hands to take. I can take, and I am compelled by deeper forces to take- forces that even I don't comprehend. But you cannot take."

So, our heroine turned and left the clearing, but could not find her way back to the Queen. The forest didn't seem the same anymore; the trees grew denser and denser, and the branches and brambles and grasses and roots and every other growing thing began to grow stronger and thicker at every turn, until our heroine was quite lost, unable to see even a foot in front of her face.

And then, the denseness was gone- the tangles faded and opened up, and she saw a great wonder. It was a cavern, deep underground, but a cavern that was full of unbelievable color, light, and beauty. The light was coming from countless gems in the walls, of every hue and size and shape. They seemed to radiate their own light, and the cavern went on forever, full of riches and beauty. The girl remained in this place forever."

* * *

This story- quite tragic, in most respects- is still layered with meaning, and would be valuable from a divinatory perspective for nearly any question. It contains enough material for many prognostications. It is a story of a human not able to overcome the many Fateful troubles that she encounters in either the human world or the Fayerie-world, but who still ends up happy in another sense, in a place of bounty and beauty, even though it is far from where she might have expected she would end up. Such is the nature of Fateful powers and life.

In this story, the heroine's misfortune cannot be solved through appeals to wisdom, nor to appeals to the powers and beings of the world itself- the powers of those places cannot answer her. Only the source of her troubles can and does school her about her limits, which leads her away from her quests and to a surprisingly positive place- though it is clear that this whole story is a death-narrative.

When doing these story readings, there are truly two main "frameworks" for interpreting the results. The first is in seeing a story that shows how a situation is going to turn out- how it goes from the time of the question, to a stated time in the future ("How shall this situation play out in the next two months?") The second is in seeing a story that offers the best advice your Divining Familiar can give you regarding how to deal with a difficult situation or person or the like.

If the story of Jeannie (example story one) was read only for advice, the following "advice pieces" can be extrapolated from it: 1. In this hardship (symbolized by

Jeannie's poverty) seek advice from a wise person or persons on clearing away major troubles. 2. Do not imagine that repeating previous efforts or tactics will help you (the ten of clubs/trees- the great forest of exhausted efforts.) 3. Be prepared to explore, alone if needs be, and take risks. It is okay to accept the generosity of others; it leads good places ultimately. 4. When facing hardships, try to grasp the role you play in generating and suffering those hardships. Try to trust more than you do.

VI. The Characters that Spring from the Cards

When you draw "face" cards, they can represent the appearance in your story of their most potent person- the supernatural figure associated with each card, as told earlier- or they can be those entities, disguised as human beings or animals, of course. But they can also be ordinary inhabitants of the spirit or human world, as governed by the list below:

King of Spades: Captain, General, Traveling magistrate or judge, Master of a school or institution, Famed scholar, Hangman or executioner, Adversarial sorcerer or male witch.

Queen of Spades: Adversarial sorceress or female witch, Shrewish woman, Wicked noblewoman with entourage.

Jack of Spades: A Soldier, a Knight, a Mercenary, a Troop of soldiers, a Highwayman, a Robber, a Murderer, a Bullbeggar, Malicious Redcap, or Fayerie Soul-Hunter.

King of Hearts: Wise man, Kindly older man, Hermit, Mendicant, a Bishop or influential cleric, a Doctor, a Mystic or Miracle-worker, a counselor or advisor.

Queen of Hearts: Beautiful woman, a Woman with reputed powers of healing or other mystical abilities, a Prostitute, the Young and beautiful wife or daughter of a King or Nobleman with her entourage.

Jack of Hearts: Wandering troubadour, Charming rogue, Magician/Illusionist, Juggler, Healer, Performer, Artist, Rakehell

King of Clubs: A Wild Animal tamer, a Foreign king or prince, a Good or ambiguous Outlaw chief or leader, a Good or ambiguous Sorcerer or male witch, a Leader of some sort, a Foreign man, a Native chieftain.

Queen of Clubs: A Foreign Queen or princess, a Good or ambiguous sorceress or female witch, a Foreign woman, a Native chieftainess or Queen.

Jack of Clubs: An Adventurer, a Scout, Outdoorsman, or Woodlands guide, an Explorer, a Ranger, a Hunter, an Outlaw, a Traveling man, a Hobb, a Wild-man of the forest.

King of Diamonds: A Wealthy merchant with entourage and traveling company, a Powerful banker or statesman, a Great Landowner or lord of a manor. A wealthy man. A leader of a funeral procession, a doctor or professor of great fame.

Queen of Diamonds: A Mother (with children, or searching for lost children), an Abbess, a Wealthy woman traveling with entourage, an Independent or influential woman (whether wealthy or not), a Harvest Queen or May Queen.

Jack of Diamonds: A Peddler, a Small-time merchant, a Beggar, a Mason, a Tradesman, a tinker, a craftsman, a Farmer, a Gambler, a Con-man.

* * *

It may be that when you perform a story reading, the first card in your first three drawn cards is a face card- a king, queen, or jack. This indicates that they may be the subject or main character of the story if you desire it- though whether they will be protagonistic or antagonistic is divined from their character card. In general, negative cards make them into antagonists, but this doesn't always have to be the case. If the Joker or the Thief is drawn as the first card, they simply modify the card that comes after them as you'd expect, and that modified card becomes the first card-station of the story.

The Joker or the Thief can come first in a batch of three cards, and end up modifying a character. For instance, in a story that begins with the Thief as the first card, and the King of Spades as the second card (let us say his character card is the Ace of Spades)- we have a very dark situation: the malevolent power modifies the King of Spades, (who in this story will be a human sorcerer) who is already motivated to kill someone or bring about some kind of dramatic change, as the ace of spades indicates. This makes his motivation a very dark one, a killing of jealousy, or a pernicious one- even a genocidal one.

If the Joker had come first, the sorcerer's motivation to kill would have been to bring about justice or protect someone, or his motivation could have been to bring about a very good change, to protect someone or some place. Remember that the Thief really "warps" and "reverses" the persons of the deck. The generous King of Diamonds or King of Coins becomes very greedy with the Thief as his character card. The Queen of Hearts or Queen of Desires becomes a very hateful figure under the Thief's influence, and so forth. Of course, a character card of blockage (like the three of clubs) can "block" a person's character- the three of clubs can block the generosity of the King of Coins, making him greedy or stingy. Consider the possibilities of the cards in these ways, when they relate to characters.

VII. The Atmosphere of the Tale

Count up how many of each suit appears in your tale or your reading- if one of the four suits has more cards in the reading than any of the others, the "atmosphere" or general tone of the entire tale is known from that suit.

If two or three suits are tied for dominance, and the last card of the reading belongs to one of the competing suits, that suit wins, and the reading is of that suit's atmosphere. If the suit of the final card does not help, then the tale's atmosphere is determined by which suit had more face cards (kings, queens, jacks) in the tale than any other. If they have the same amount of face cards, the atmosphere of the tale is determined by which had higher ranking face cards- a king beats a jack, and so forth. If this does not beat the tie, the atmosphere of the story is "muddled"- it is mixed, shared between the tied suits. But this can reveal something special, as is described below.

The "character cards" drawn for characters in the story do not count towards determining the atmosphere of the tale.

Reading is predominantly Spades or Elf-Arrows: **Spiteful Atmosphere**. Spiteful tales are governed from within by Fates of conflict and hurt, challenge and stress, competition and anxiety. Stormy weather is more common in these tales, as is betrayal.

Reading is predominantly Hearts or Desires: **Venusian Atmosphere**. The Venusian tale, the love-tale, the romantic story, or the "tales of silk and velvet" do not have to be positive or heartwarming in any manner, nor end well- but they will be ruled from within by Fates of attraction and yearning (which can lead to very strange and unexpected outcomes) and desire for pleasure, and the machinations of allies, lovers, and friends. Twilight and cool evenings, lazy autumn days, or fresh spring days are more common in these tales, as well as lust and delight as a major motivation.

Reading is predominantly Clubs or Trees: **Adventuring Atmosphere**. The Adventure tale is ruled from within by Fates of restlessness, exploration, expansion, and interaction- the many possibilities of interaction that can emerge when friends, strangers, and all other kinds of characters interact and affect one another. Something is sought in any tale, the adventure tale posits a supreme prize for cunning or brave interaction more than most. These are tales of either hard winter or high summer, when adventurers set out for long journeys or face challenges, and they often contain the element of triumph over adversity- or epic defeat.

Reading is predominantly Diamonds or Coins: **Hearthside Atmosphere**. The hearthside tale is ruled by the Fates of a house, or a particular family, or small group of people. It is ruled by the Fates of a local place, a small forest or farm known only to a few. Unlike the other tales that can involve distant lands, the hearthside tale is about something that happened nearby, perhaps a long time ago. It is about a family and their relationship to a local community or the land or the spirits of the same.

It is a tale of mid-winter or spring cleaning, of summer festivities or autumn coolness, with the common element of discovery and either making one's home and family or friends more secure and strong, or discovering threats to the same. They are about becoming more of a part of a place, or discovering the "universe within the small fenced-in yard."

Muddled atmospheres make statements: A Spiteful Venusian atmosphere presages troubles in love or relationships; a Venusian Adventure atmosphere reveals a special nuance to the adventure, or what inspires it or causes it; a Spiteful Hearthside tale speaks to trouble in a home or family or property, and so forth.

In general, Spiteful tales are ill omens, and presage trying times. Venusian tales are ambiguous, always with risks of fortunes changing, even when they are good stories. Adventure tales are positive omens and can have far-reaching implications, and Hearthside tales are generally comfortable and positive, if a bit small-scale. They don't presage long-term life changes.

No fortune or misfortune gained from a Spiteful tale will be long lasting, such is the airy nature of the spades/elf-arrows- but misfortunes will still probably be the longer lasting of the two. Fortunes and misfortunes gained in Venusian tales- the suit of desires, which is a watery suit, are slippery and unreliable or unstable a good portion of the time.

Fortunes and misfortunes gained from Adventure tales are reliably lasting like a steady fire with much fuel, but can be "attacked" or overcome by counter-forces. Fortunes and misfortunes gained or presaged by earthy Hearthside tales are ordinarily very long lasting.

In sample reading two, we find that of the nine cards drawn, three were hearts, and three were clubs. The ending card is a diamond, so it doesn't help us determine the atmosphere, but the hearts suit had a king, and the highest the club suit had was a queen, so the story has a Venusian atmosphere. The close call we had between the hearts and clubs was resolved in the favor of the hearts or desires, but the tale still has elements of an adventure.

VIII. "YES" and "NO" for Those Who Must Know

Unlike many other oracles, this one can be utilized to answer questions that have yes or no answers, though I do not suggest this method be utilized much. Its matrix is too simple for the complex situations of life that we are always facing, so use it sparingly, or only in emergencies, and only if one has a deep and close relationship to a Divining Familiar.

Spades- Elf Arrows- mean "No."
Hearts- Desires- mean "Yes."
Clubs- Trees- mean "Perhaps No." (Inclining towards no)
Diamonds- Coins- means "Perhaps Yes." (Inclining towards yes)

Draw three cards after your cut, and look at the suits. "Yes" and "No" cards cancel each other out, and "Perhaps No" and "Perhaps Yes" cards cancel one another out. See what is left in your reading after the cancellations have occurred. That is your answer.

Examples:

Ace of Hearts + Seven of Clubs + King of Spades: *Yes, Perhaps No, and No*. Yes and No cancel, leaving behind "Perhaps No." The answer is "probably not" or "inclining towards no."

Three of Diamonds + Queen of Hearts + Ace of Hearts: *Perhaps Yes, Yes, and Yes*. The answer is Yes.

Eight of Spades + Six of Diamonds + Jack of Clubs: *No, Perhaps Yes, Perhaps No*. Perhaps Yes and Perhaps No cancel, leaving behind No. Answer is No.

King of Hearts, Two of Spades, Nine of Hearts: *Yes, No, Yes*. The Yes and No cancel, leaving behind, "Yes." The answer is Yes.

In this method, the Joker is the equivalent of a heart, a strong yes, and the Thief is the equivalent of a spade, a strong no.

If you get no cards that cancel- like two clubs and a heart- a "maybe no, maybe no, and a yes"- the two maybe no's "join together" to form a strong no, and then, they together cancel out that heart's "yes." Such a reading is an inconclusive answer- it means "this situation can go either way; the answer isn't yes or no." It may also mean "not possible to answer in this way" or "unable to know at this time."

The same would be true if you had two diamonds and a spade- the two "maybe yes" cards form together a strong yes, which then cancels the spade's "no", leaving the inconclusive result.

IX. Time and the Cards

There are 52 cards in a deck, and 52 weeks in a year. With spades/elf arrows representing winter, and starting with ace (1) and going down to the king (13), you have the card that belongs to the first week of winter, all the way down to the 13th week of winter. Hearts/desires represent autumn, clubs/trees represent spring, and diamonds/coins represent summer. By pulling one card, you get a certain week of the year. By pulling two, you get a range- the Seven of Hearts and the Seven of Clubs in a pair say "between the seventh week of autumn and the seventh week of spring."

Jokers and Thieves are never used in timing readings.

Each of the suits gives a sense of speed, and a time-range, all by themselves. Consult the following table:

* * *

Spades: Very soon, or Sooner than you'd like. Also, "not very long."

Clubs: Not long from now, within the next few weeks or months. Also, "a short to moderate amount of time."

Heart: A few months to a year or two. Also, "a moderate to lengthy amount of time."

Diamonds: Not for a very long time, or simply "a very long time."

* * *

It may help to "feel" the time-prognostication of suits by looking at them with regards to a century. Within a framework of 100 years, a spade means "this year." A club means "not this year, not next year, but sometime in this decade." A heart means "maybe 30-40 years from now" and a diamond means "90-100 years from now."

X. Oracular Pronouncements

It is possible to receive direct oracular "sentences" or pronouncements from the Divining Familiar or source of your readings. You can also do this after you have done a reading, to get further insights into the situation, or get further advice on how to handle any challenges the reading may have presented to you or a querent. This is done by randomizing by your ordinary method, and drawing out five cards, from which a sentence is created. Many examples are given here.

When using this method, the King of Diamonds also gains the meaning "Man", the Queen of Diamonds gains the meaning "Woman", and the Jack of Diamonds gains the meaning "Child" or "New." The Thief means "bad" or "lie" or "trickery", and the Joker means "good", "help" or "improvement." Here are some examples:

* * *

1. Five Cards Drawn: Ace of Spades, Two of Spades, King of Hearts, Queen of Hearts, Ten of Clubs

Meanings: Change, fight, understanding, love, exhausted

"Change your understanding of this conflict; love is exhausted (or finished) here."

* * *

2. Five Cards Drawn: The Thief, Five of Hearts, Seven of Spades, Nine of Spades, Six of Spades

Meanings: Bad, heartbreak, delay, regret, caution

"A bad heartbreak or sadness is delayed: you will regret being cautious right now."

* * *

3. Five Cards Drawn: Eight of Diamonds, King of Diamonds, Four of Diamonds, Jack of Clubs, Jack of Spades

Meanings: Assurance, man, stability, risk, misfortune

"The man can assure you of stability, but a significant risk of misfortune is here."

* * *

4. Five Cards Drawn: Three of Diamonds, Eight of Hearts, Ten of diamonds, Four of Spades, Two of Clubs

Meanings: Acquisition, loyalty, many, peace, agreement

"You have acquired loyalty in this situation, and many agreements that will secure peace for you."

* * *

5. Five Cards Drawn: Three of Spades, Jack of Hearts, Queen of Clubs, Eight of Clubs, Two of Hearts
Meanings: Injury, lover, connection, wisdom, negotiation (or exchange)

A connection you have with a lover causes you an injury, which leads to a wise negotiation (or exchange)"

* * *

6: Five Cards Drawn: Nine of Diamonds, King of Clubs, Five of Spades, Seven of Diamonds, Ace of Hearts

Meanings: Abundance/power, protection, mortal injury, disappointment, (lonely) heart

"Abundant protection from the mortal injury of a disappointed heart."

In this last example, if this was you asking for advice about a situation, the oracle is saying "You're about to need a lot of protection from the hurt, disappointed heart of someone."

That's if you were asking for advice. If you were asking what was going to come of, say, a betrayal you were just caught in, this says that your relationship will not be ending: you are protected from the "mortal injury of the disappointed heart" of your partner. It may not be nice at first, but under "abundant protection", you probably won't be losing the relationship. But you'd be foolish to imagine a "mortal injury" means that things can ever really be the same.

XI. Whispers of the Soul

The basic "three card reading" only allows for the Divining Familiar or the Soul itself to whisper a single line to you- so it is best assayed when you quickly need to know "What forces are about to arise around (so-and-so) situation in the near future?"

Randomize and then cut the deck, and turn over the top three cards. Kings, Queens, and Jacks will not receive a "character card" in this reading. Divine from the three cards you see what the situation will be like soon, or what you should do immediately.

What shall come of my mother's surgery, with regard to the health of her body? (Worried that the doctors said she could emerge from it permanently incapacitated.) Draw: Seven of Clubs, Queen of Clubs, Two of Clubs: Frustration, Achievement, Constructive Effort. This might be interpreted as some loss of physical ability, but not as much as feared, and with a further chance to mitigate what was lost with therapy, or regain it. Or, a sentence can be constructed from the reading's meanings: "There will be frustration in achieving productive effort."

What shall come of my friend's desire to attempt the very dangerous bike-path down the mountain, which though exciting, is only suggested for very advanced bikers? Draw: Two of Hearts, Six of Spades, Three of Spades. Friendly Exchange or Negotiation, Safe path, Wound. This shows that the friend will do fine, find the way down nearly the entire way safely, but become injured somehow before the end. A sentence constructed from the meanings would say "Exchanging safety for a wound"-

surely a humorous way of suggesting they not try it just now.

What will come of it if I attempt this sorcerous work to manipulate this person's heart into submission? Draw: Ace of Diamonds, King of Clubs, Seven of Diamonds. Opportunity to Gain, Leadership, Disappointment/Despair. The conditions are right for your work to succeed, you will succeed at first, but the final result will be disappointment or worse- their hearts cannot be contained or tamed long. A sentence made from these keywords? "A chance to lead the dance of disappointment" or "an opportunity which leads to disappointment."

XII. Death Letter

Only very strange people actually want to know how much longer they have to live, these days. In the off chance that you care to know such a dangerous thing- for it can surely destroy peace of mind in most modern people, as readily as it can grant it- and if you are certain that you have a divining familiar or trustworthy source for the divination, the following process is suggested.

Assume that you will die at age 80. Many people may live beyond that point, but for this divination, assume that 80 will be the age you die. If you are already 80, this procedure changes a bit, as mentioned below.

Subtract your current age from 80, which will yield a certain number of years. Then, following your ordinary divination procedure, draw a single card. Look at the suit.

If you draw a spade, it means that you have 10-20% of those years remaining- meaning that you can die before that time, of course, but you likely won't live beyond that range of years. A 40-year-old man drawing the Jack of Spades is seeing a divination that forecasts his death within 4-8 years. Further, if the spade drawn was an ace or a jack, this foretells the possibility of an accident, illness, or injury taking one's life before that allotted time. Low results for young people must always presage death by accident, injury, or unexpected illness, one way or the other.

If you wish to get even more specific, after you have seen your "death age suit", turn over another card, and see if it is black or red. If it's red, you can be relatively certain that your "percentage" is in the high end of the spectrum (18-

20%.) But if it's black, your percentage is in the low end (10-15%)

If you draw a club, it means that you have 40-60% of those years remaining. The 40-year-old man is seeing that he will likely die within 16-24 years. If the club drawn is a jack, this portends the possibility of an accident or injury taking one's life before those years are up.

If you draw a heart, it means that you have 75-80% of those years remaining. The 40-year-old man is seeing 30-32 more years, and with hearts, chances are very good that he'll make it that long. The chance of early death by accident or injury is too small at this point to be read about, even though nothing can ever be ruled out completely.

If you draw a diamond, it means that you have 90-100% of those years remaining, and possibly that you will live beyond 80. The 40-year-old man is seeing 36-40 more years of life almost assuredly, but the possibility exists that he will surpass that.

Such is the nature of advancements in health and technology, at least in the first world, that people who are between the ages of 18 and 30 at present may be better served subtracting their age from 90, instead of 80, before doing this divination.

I do not suggest this reading be done for anyone below the age of 18, for the Fates of an adult life are not yet layered upon that person and set, so there is much uncertainty and unclearness. Truthfully, even for age 18- itself a culturally constructed, and rather arbitrarily chosen "age" for adulthood- the same is true. This method is most effective for those who have some adult years of life under their belt. If I was forced to read for a very young child, I would subtract their age from 100 to obtain the reading.

If you are already 80 years old, or older, subtract your age from 100, and draw your card. Spades mean 25% of those years in the range you obtained are likely the amount you have left; clubs mean 50% of those years; hearts mean 75% of those years, and Diamonds mean you may likely make it to 100 years of age.

XIII. The Table of Major Suit Associations

This table represents a minor divination system by itself. Its intended use is to offer clues, extra information, or insights into perplexing situations or interpretations that may have arisen from other readings, but a clever person can see how this table might be used to offer clues as to how a person may die, to find lost objects or persons, or many other things.

To gain information from this table, the process is simplicity itself: randomize in your ordinary way, cut once, and turn over the first card. This tells you the suit. The next card tells you the number: an Ace is "1", and all of the other numbered cards are the number they indicate. A Jack is 11, a Queen is 12, and a King is 13. Thus, if you got King of Spades, followed by the Queen of Hearts, your reading from the table is found under "Things of the Elf-Arrows" and "12", which is "Anxiety."

You may turn over up to six cards per reading from this table, for a total of three entries gained from it. The entries should be read together, for whatever insight they may offer. Bear in mind that the associations conjured by these entries are as important as the entries themselves. "Suicide" may indicate despair or hopelessness. "Hospitals or places of therapy or healing" may indicate things getting better, or recovery. "Valleys, canyons, low places" can mean depression or low luck, as well as it can mean anything else from an actual valley, to a place below one's notice or attention. These hints and clues born of the table should be read on more than one level.

* * *

Elf-Arrows (Spades, Northward)

(1) Winds, storms, (2) Breathing, breath and breathing related problems, (3) Anger, courts, government places and military posts (4) Places of learning and knowledge (5) Accidents, (6) Cuts, surgeries (7) Suicide, (8) Violence, fights, (9) Divorces, (10) Injuries, (11) Threats, thefts, crimes (12) Anxiety, (13) Heights, the sky, deserts, mountain peaks

Desires (Hearts, Westward)

(1) Waters and watery places, boats and harbors (2) Emotions, dreams (3) Eye, vision(s), hallucinations (4) Mental Illnesses (5) Nervous system, (6) Biological fluids and blood, hospitals, places of therapy or healing (7) Fears, (8) Longings, desires (9) Moodiness, (10) Circulation, (11) Intoxication, confusion (12) Diseases of tissues, (13) The heart, places of religion

Trees (Clubs, Eastward)

(1) Meetings, (2) Work, tasks, assignments, (3) Art, places of culture, parks (4) Projects, (5) Crafts, (6) Bones, joints, (7) Bodily energy, willpower, (8) Travel, (9) Forests, plains, wastelands, (10) Motivation, ambition, obsession (11) Beasts, sports, places of social gathering (12) Growths and tumors (13) Burns and fires, pollutions

Coins (Diamonds, Southward)

(1) Money, savings, treasures, markets (2) Heirlooms, (3) Property, home (4) Gardens, food, nutrition, (5) Houses, buildings, (6) Graves, cemeteries (7) Fields/solitude/lonely

(8) Mountains, hills, (9) Valleys, canyons, low places (10) Old age, slow degeneration, (11) Deafness, (12) Senility, (13) Immobilization, incapacitation

Appendix: Chart of Basic Card Meanings

	Spades	Hearts	Clubs	Diamonds
King	Severe, Merciless Vengeance, Justice	Wisdom, Good Counsel, Understanding	Leadership, Protection, Vitality	Wealth, Generosity
Queen	Difficulty, Criticism Anxiety	Allure, Love, Pleasure, Addiction	Achievement, Connection	Abundance, Nurturing
Jack	Enemy, Treachery Misfortune	Seduction, Manipulation, Lover	Adventure, Risk, Guidance	Gamble, Irresponsible, Unpredictable
Ace	Death, Change	Lonely Heart, or, New Love or Passion	Solitude, Urge to Explore	A coin, a letter, Opportunity to gain, news or message
Two	Duel, Fight, Dispute	Sex, Interaction, Friendship, Negotiation, Exchange	Productive Effort, Ally, Pact, Agreement	Exchange, Transactions, Choices, Gossip or Rumors
Three	Wound, Injury	Stable Love, Stable Relationship, Beauty	Hedge, Wall, Obstacle, Blockage	Job, Acquisition, Employment, Means to gain, Greed
Four	Peace (perhaps fragile)	Boredom, Decrease, Cooling	Clearing, Field, Openness, Harvest, Reaping	Table, Stability, Store/Shop, Unchanging
Five	Mortal Injury, Lethal Hurt	Heartbreak, Sadness	Failure	Poverty, Want, Loss, Ugliness
Six	Safe Path, Caution Movement, Travel, Change	The Rose Road- Happy Progress, Fruitful Relations, Flow, Inspiration, Change	Path through the Forest, Progress, Movement, Guidance, Learning	Golden Road- Sustenance, Provision, Plenty
Seven	Delayed, Stuck Hard Choice	Wavering, Disquiet, Depression, Untrusting, Betrayal	Indecision, Confusion, Frustration.	Disappointment, Despair, Theft
Eight	Frozen, Imprisoned, Trapped	Healthy, Strong Relationship, Loyalty, Well-Being	Wisdom, Expertise, Achievement, Honors	Castle, Sturdiness, Assurance, Strength, Defense, Safety, Secrets
Nine	Funeral Road, Coffin, Regrets, Endings	Birth, Wedding, Happiness, Union, Alliance	Thicket, Loss of Clarity, Obstacle	Abundance, Power, Authority
Ten	Graveyard, Battlefield, Ruin, Decay, Desolation, Greed	Rose Queen's Bower: Dreams, Comfort, Bliss	Rest, Spent, Exhaustion, Limitation	Cavern of Precious Stones- Endless Bounty, Wonder, A horde, much, many.

About the Author

Robin Artisson is a modern day practitioner of traditional sorcery and divination, a social critic, folklorist, scholar of pre-Christian religions, and proponent of spiritual ecology. He is the author of several noted works on those topics.

Printed in Great Britain
by Amazon